ACCOLAY

I0165891

CONERTO No. 1

in A minor

FOR VIOLIN AND PIANO

(JOSEF GINGOLD)

Published in 2019 by Allegro Editions

Concerto No. 1 for Violin and Piano
ISBN: 978-1-9748-9955-5 (paperback)

Cover design by Kaitlyn Whitaker

Cover image: "Music Sheet" by danielo courtesy of
Shutterstock; "Violin Front View Isolated on White"
by AGCuesta courtesy of Shutterstock

ALLEGRO
EDITIONS

2

CONCERTO

in A minor
for Violin and Piano*

Edited by JOSEF GINGOLD

JEAN BATISTE ACCOLAY
(1845-1910)

Allegro moderato

*Originally for Violin and Orchestra.

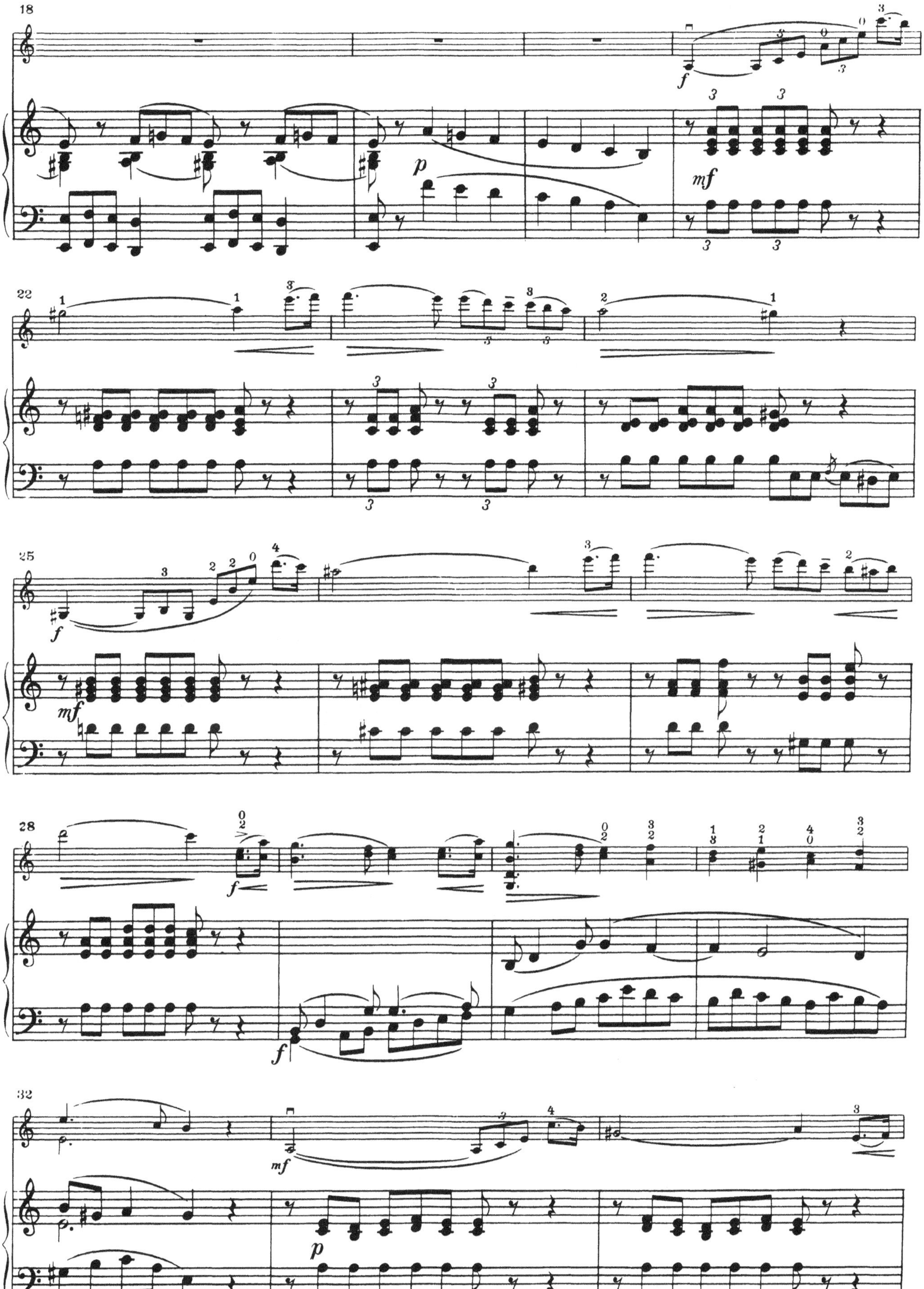
18
f
p
mf
22
25
f
mf
28
f
f
32
mf
p

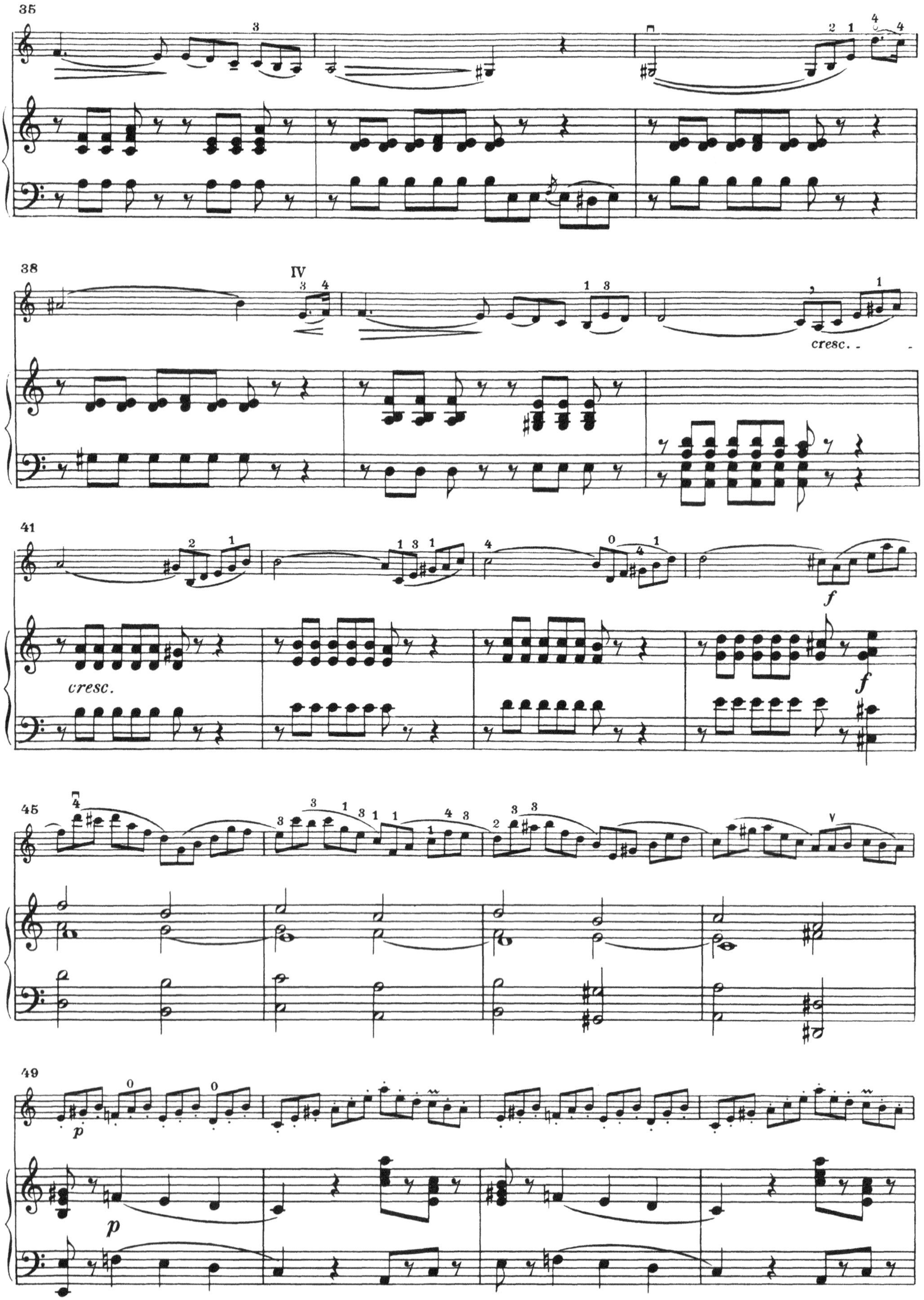
35
38
IV
cresc.
41
cresc.
f
45
49
p

cresc.
f
cresc.
f
poco a poco rit.
a tempo
p con espressione
cantabile
a tempo
p
cresc.
cresc.

cresc.
cresc.
f largamente
colla parte
a tempo
mf a tempo
cresc.
cresc.

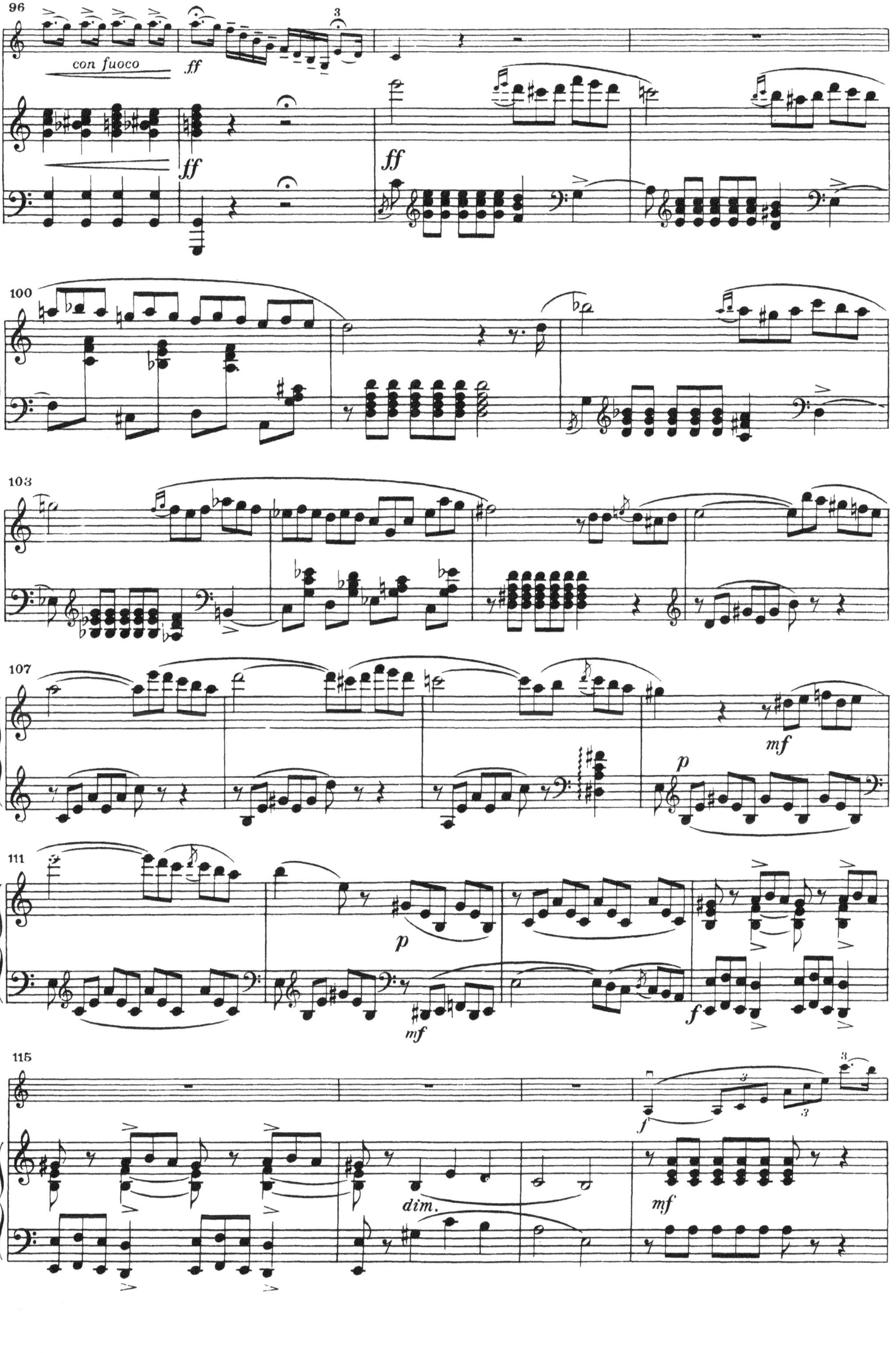
96
con fuoco
ff
ff
ff
100
103
107
p
mf
111
p
mf
f
115
dim.
f
mf

119
122
mf
125
cresc.
cresc.
129
largamente e ritenuto
ff
ff colla parte
133. a tempo
p a tempo
ten.
ten.

137
pp
ten.
140 ten.
cresc.
cresc.
143
f
f
146
p
p
cresc.
cresc.
150
f poco a poco rit.
f poco a poco rit.

Maggiore
p a tempo
cantabile
p a tempo
cresc.
cresc.
p
p
f largamente
fp a tempo
cresc.
f colla parte
p a tempo

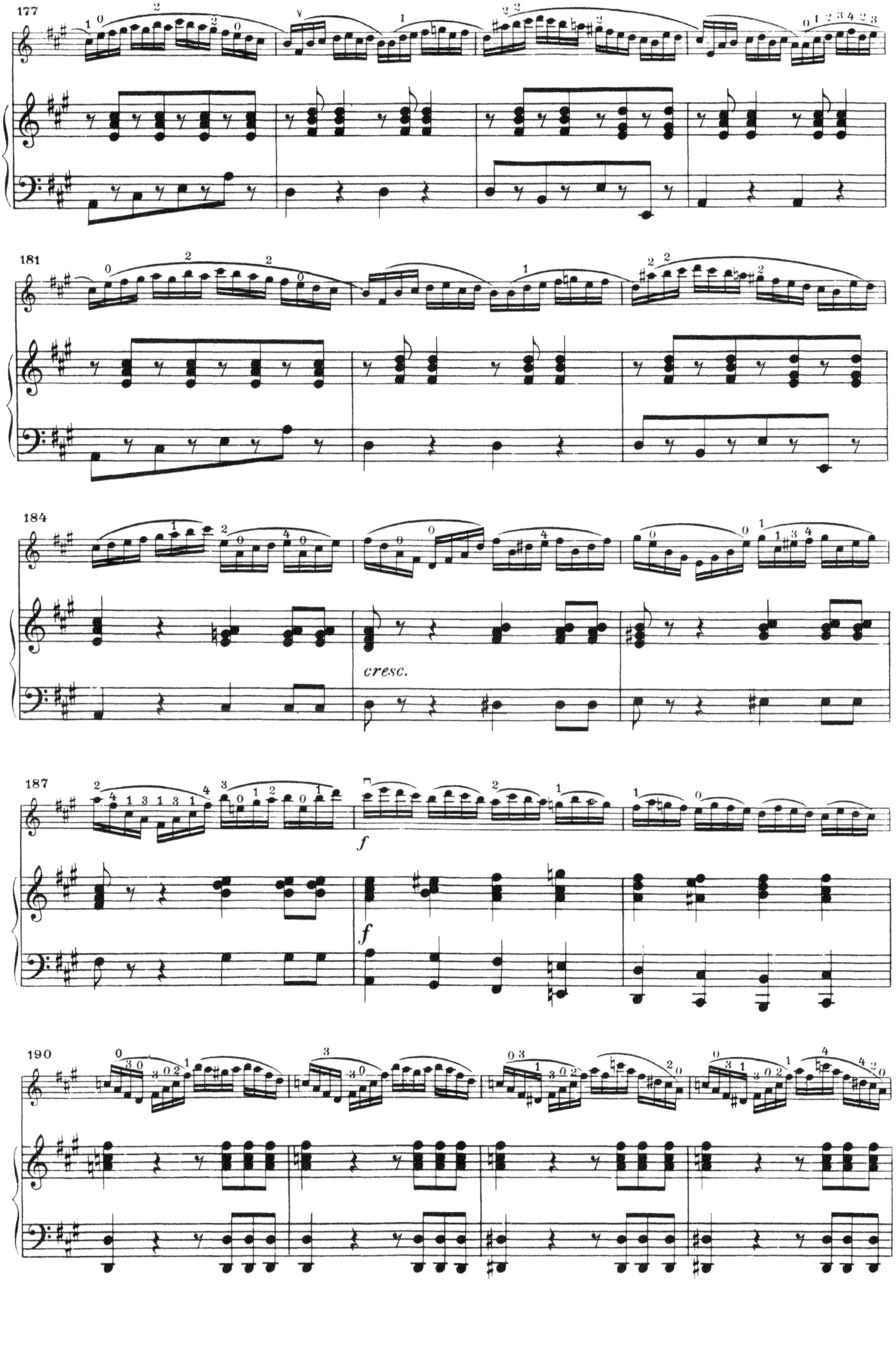
177
181
184
cresc.
187
f
f
190

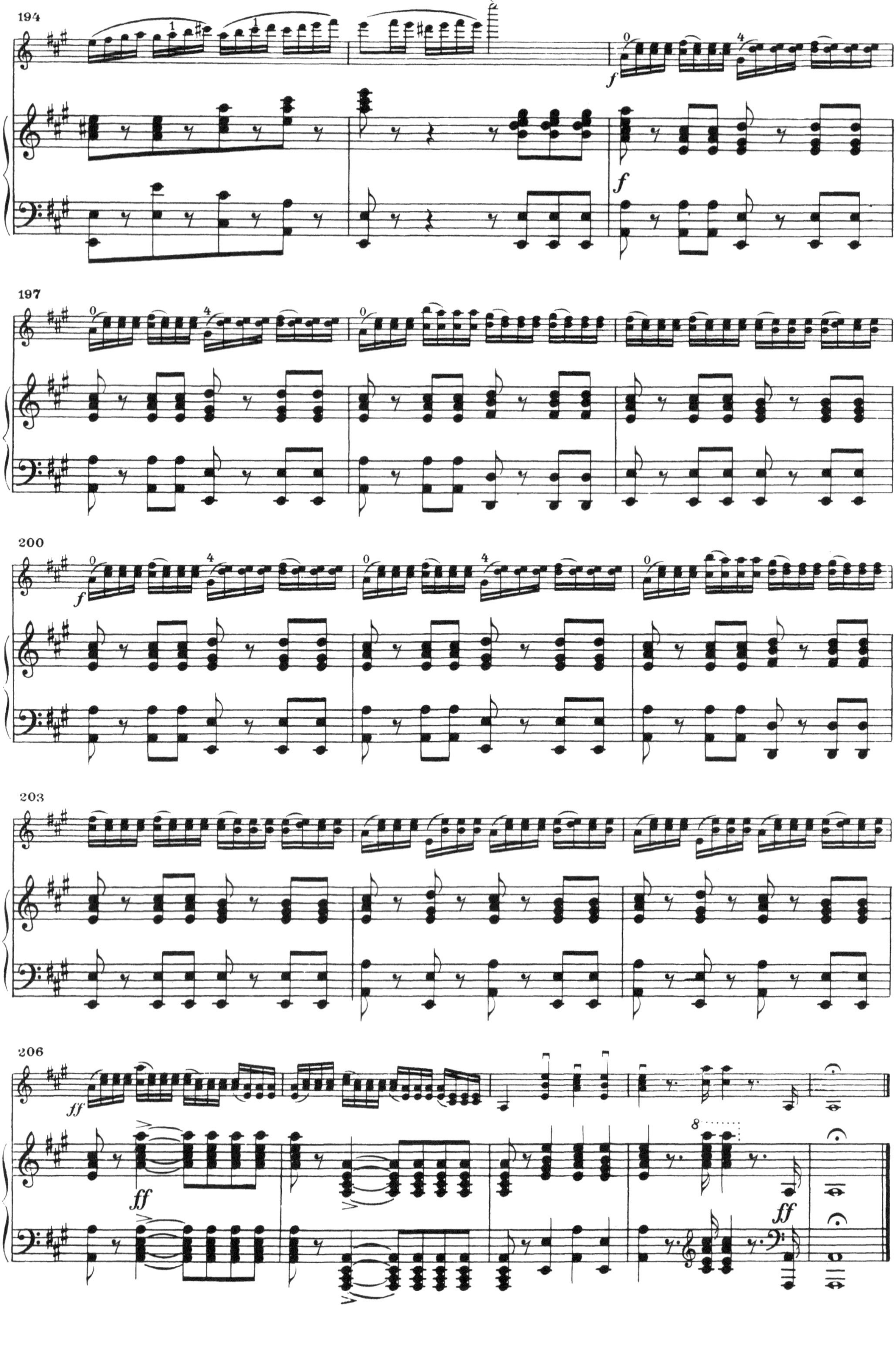
194
197
200
203
206

CONCERTO No. 1

in A minor

VIOLIN

CONCERTO

in A minor
for Violin and Piano*

VIOLIN

Edited by JOSEF GINGOLD

JEAN BATISTE ACCOLAY
(1845-1910)

Allegro moderato

*Originally for Violin and Orchestra.

a tempo
p con espressione
cantabile
II
I
cresc.
p
cresc.
f largamente
a tempo
f
(2 1 2 1)
p con grazia
cresc.
f
con fuoco
ff
17

cresc.
largamente e ritenuto
ten.
ten.
ten.
ten.
cresc.
cresc.
poco a poco rit.
Maggiore
a tempo
cantabile
cresc.

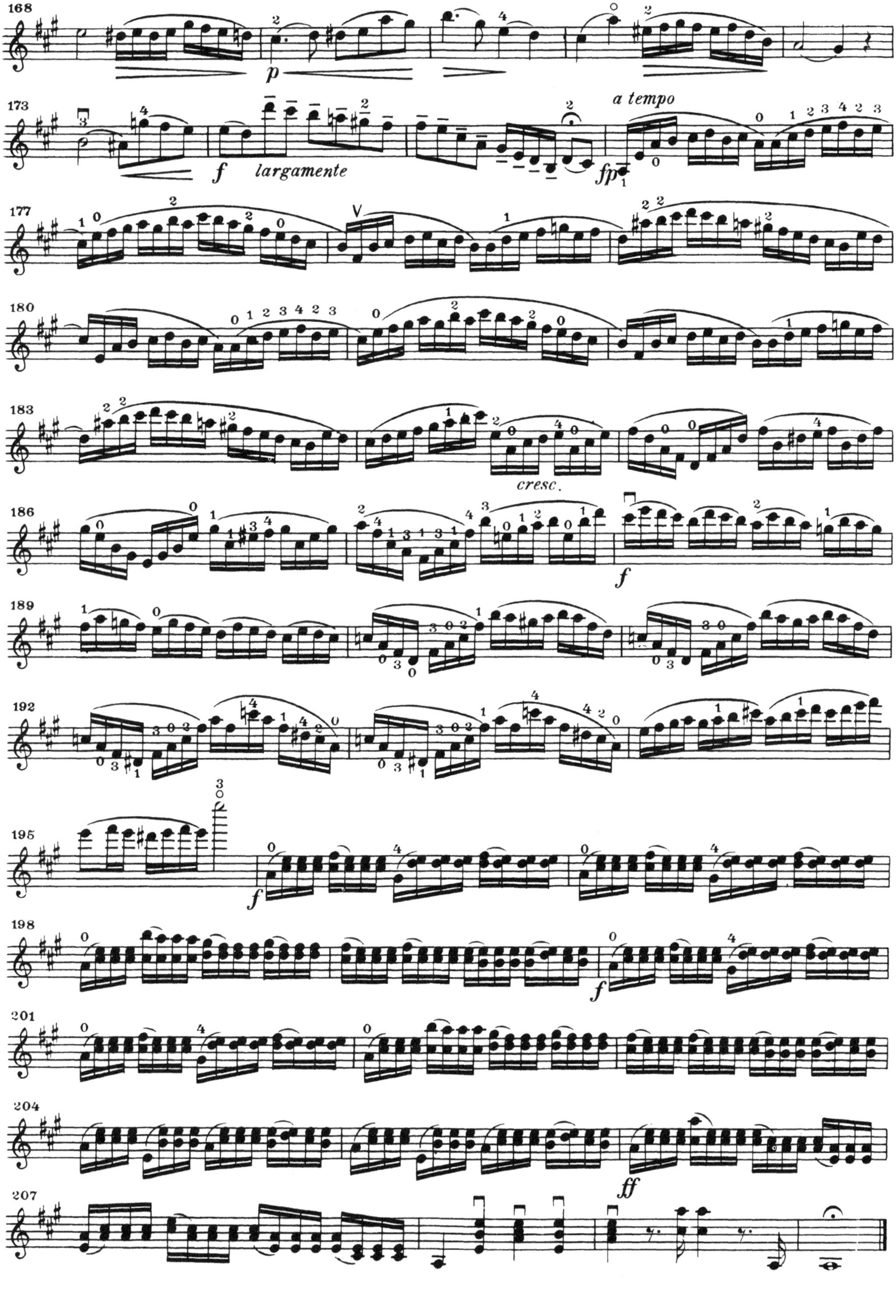
p
f
largamente
a tempo
fp
cresc.
f
f
f
ff

www.ingramcontent.com/pod-product-compliance
Lightning Source LLC
Chambersburg PA
CBHW080537090426
42733CB00015B/2611